APOCALY

Tony Langham
Apocalypse Soup

sfp
small fry press

First Published in Great Britain in 2000 by
Small Fry Publications
1 Eton Terrace, Mytholmroyd , West Yorkshire, HX7 5JH.
e-mail: Langhamfamily@losgringos.fsnet.co.uk
Printed in England by Arc & Throstle Press, Todmorden.

ISBN 0 946407 99 1

Cover Illustration by Mercedes Langham-Lopez, Aged 7.
With thanks to Jordan Langham–Lopez for editing and formatting.

CONTENTS

Para Silvia, mi esposa, mi amiga, mi amante
- las Trinidad Sagrada de mi corazon

'What we are today comes from our thoughts
of yesterday, and our present thoughts
build our life of tomorrow; our life
is the creation of our mind.
If a man acts or speaks with an impure
mind, suffering follows him as the wheel of
the cart follows the beast that draws the cart!'

The Dhammapada.

RIVER MEMORY

Thirty years ago
we caught chub on this stretch.
big fish, as long as my forearm,
voracious feeders, unable
to resist the chrysalis
my brother and I dapped
downstream in the afternoon sun.

We stood barefoot then, thigh-deep
in mid-river, bracing ourselves
against the current. Used
no floats. It was all a question
of touch that day,
of fingering the line as it rippled
off the spool.

Each bite was the same.
There was no finesse. Water
swirled line tightened
and we struck, setting
the hook, our rod-tips arching
downwards, as if suddenly
divining the water we stood in.

Played slowly so they would not break
the surface, thrash and throw the hook,
they came like supplicants, one by one,
mouths agape, to the net.

Carried to the bank they lay still,
exhausted, while we worked the hooks
from each gawping mouth,
before returning them
to the river's benediction
and watched as they slipped away,
riding the lithe currents,
seeking sanctuary downstream.

Twenty then, fifty now,
I watch my sons fish the same stretch,
their expectations overcoming inexperience,
catching finger-length gudgeon
on small hooks
tied using a knot my
brother taught me.

He should be here to show them
the others Time has unravelled
in my memory. But continents
divide us. Rivers,
seas, oceans.

Thirty years of silence.
No letters. No calls. No reasons.
Time enough for Love to fade.
Time enough to forget,
But my hook is too well set
And the river flows

Ceaselessly. Ceaselessly.

PARTY, PARTY

Ginsberg's in a corner with Basho,
They're drinking sweet rice wine;
Monk vamps, Chet and Bird blow,
The music's cool, so fine.

Fitzgerald's standing at the bar,
Drinking with Hemingway;
Willie Blake's tight with a seraphim,
They're talking Judgement Day.

Sinatra's schmoozing with Dean Martin,
With Sammy and the Rat Pack;
Warhol's hanging with Dellasandro
Burrough's cruising with Kerouac.

Sam Beckett, Francis Bacon
And the Pre-Raphaelite Gang are there;
Along with Elvis and Leonardo,
Rousseau and Apollinaire.

Bogart and Brecht are playing five-card stud,
With Einstein and Lao Tze;
Watched by a straight in a Brook's Bros. suit,
Who's with the C.I.A.

'Round midnight the joint's really jumpin',
And Kafka gets down with Bardot;
Nijinski does the Soft Shoe Shuffle,
Descarte grooves with Greta Garbo.

Harpo Marx and Chico are busy
Chasing Mae West around;
But Groucho's busy writing limericks
With Eliot and Ezra Pound.

Rothko and Jackson Pollock
Are both doing their thing;
B. B. King plays some elegant riffs,
Jung reads the Tao Te Ching.

Fidel flies in from Havana,
Hands out a few cigars;
Then splits with Dylan Thomas,
To hit some Downtown bars.

Picasso moves around the room
With a Polaroid to record the scene;
Surprises Brando with Silvia Plath
And Auden with Jimmy Dean.

And I'm making out with Marilyn
Who arrived with JFK;
But Jack had to cut out early,
Mr.President couldn't play

So we sit there and I tell her,
That I really dig her the most;
And before the party's over,
We take off for the Coast.

Drive down the Pacific Highway,
In a flame-red Thunderbird,
Hit the beach as dawn comes up,
Soft light, soft breeze, soft words.

Drink champagne, smoke a while
Then turn the T-Bird and go.
Drive home as the surf's rising,
Talking about DiMaggio.

LEPIDOPTRISTESSE

We are the keepers
of their Grail, light.
Each night they come
to us, a horde
of tiny extremeists,
silk-winged Hezbollah
beating their frail bodies
against the window-pane,
seeking entry, obsessed.

They are relentless.
Were there a flame
they would burn gladly,
but in that absence
are mesmerised ,drawn
instead by the neon
intensity we sit
beneath ,drinking coffee,
undisturbed by
their quiet frenzy.

Morning will see them
gone, though not every one.
Some will remain
until the rain or wind
sweeps them away, remain
like winnowed husks
on the window ledge, spent.

STREET INCIDENT

Anyone happening upon them
would have wondered.

Two men locked together
sprawled on the pavement,
the older one
cradling the younger
in his arms.

Anyone would have wondered.
An accident perhaps?
Drunks? Homeless?

Whosowhatwhichever.
They caused passers-by
to step into the road.
An inconvenience.

Only as I closed on them
did I understand.
Saw then,the held body
in spasm, the eyes rolled backwards,
temporarily sightless
as blank
as a Greek statue's –
a *grand mal* in progress.

I should have looked away.
But as I passed
I could not avert my eyes.
Such fierce tenderness!

Frenzy in the grip of Love.
Almost allegorical,

a kind of Pieta.

INHERITANCE

After the loaves were baked
And had cooled enough to eat
My mother would take one
And before slicing it
Make the Sign of the Cross
On its underside with a knife,
Not to cut or score
The crisp, fresh crust
You understand, but merely
To touch blade to bread,
While she murmered a prayer
Of Thanksgiving for the day's
Bounty beneath her breath,
An observence taught her
By her mother, who in turn
Was taught by hers, she said.

How many generations peformed
The same small rite I cannot say
And those who might have told me,
Cannot now. All I know is, when
The loaf to hand is uncut ,before
Slicing it I make the Sign
Of the Cross on its underside
With a knife, not to cut or score
The crust you understand, but merely
To touch blade to bread
While I say a thanksgiving prayer
Beneath my breath, for the day's
Bounty, a benediction for all those
Living and all those dead, whose lives
Have leavened mine with love,
For those who made my bread.

PETIT HOMMAGE

On
a beach
in the
midday
heat

a young
woman
stands naked
attending

a minotaur
who sits
on a chair
of carved
rosewood

beneath
a saffron
canopy.

At his feet
lie scattered
spheres
of variegated
basalt

representing
the cosmology
of his dreams

and crouched
at his side
a blue arsed
mandrill
plays a lyre
for his

assembled
guests

who feast,
while acrobats
construct pyramids
and other predetermined
geometrical structures

and jugglers perform
with compliant,
iridescent fish

while clowns
enact scenes
from obscure
mythologies

composed
and recited
by a chorus
of blind poets

as Harlequin
consults
a neon tarot
and a crystal

in which
two lovers
can be seen
fucking

joyously

unaware
that their
coupling
is being painted
in precise
and magical
detail

by the famous
artist and purveyor
of multitudinous
realities

Pablo Diego
Jose Francisco
de Paula
Juan Nepomunceno
Mario de los Remedios
Crispin, Crispiano
Santisima Trinidad
Ruiz

otherwise known as

Picasso.

CINEMA VERITIE

Between musical numbers Busby Berkley
Would have sold his soul to choreograph,
A green-eyed Bollywood diva
Into heavy lip-gloss sets out to revenge
Her father who killed himself
When a business deal
With a shady partner went wrong.

In the process she tracks down,
Stalks and seduces the partner's son,
Who of course falls for her in spades.
The set-up's perfect, allowing her
To dig the dirt on her lover's father,
Whom she intends to expose,
Until she realises she really loves the son
And caught in its alchemy forgives the father

It's three ayem in the morning.
Alone again while you work
The weekend shift, I lie in bed
Watching an Indian film.
It's Dostoyevsky with dance routines.
A swirling-saffron, incense-scented,
Badly-subtitled, schlock Karma flick.
But I watch it to the end.
Even after all these years
Your absence makes sleep elusive.

As the credits roll, a midsummer
Sunrise gathers, ready to spill
Its pristine light over the crag
Behind the house.
In an hour, your shift completed,
You'll drive home, slide into bed
And warm yourself against me
As you always do
Regardless of the season.

Given a kind lens
And sensitive lighting,
We could be lovers in a film,
Finding redemption
In the simplicity of holding,
Finding shelter from the pain
Humanity trades in.
Lovers, lying silently together,
Because Time has refined
The language passing between them,
Because their Love is encoded
In every touch.

DUCKS ON HEBDEN WATER

Past masters at treading water,
They gather, buoy-buoyant below,
In expectation that my bread
Will be shared ever hopeful that between
Hand and lip, a slip will deliver
Some accidental bounty.

They lack the chic of swans
And of geese their stature,
But seem content with their lot,
Kept prosperous, kept plump
And sleek-feathered by those
Who come to feed them.

Eventually they tire of waiting,
Turn and let the forceful current
Sweep them downstream.
for the richer pickings
Cast waterward
By a gaggle of tourists

But one remains, stays
With me, her eyes bright
And optomistic.
Only now I share, tear off
A small wheaten shard
To reward her virtue.

A crumb of kindness
Is never wasted
On bird, man or beast.
With almost sacramental grace,
She lifts her head
To take the offered host
From me, her priest.

EVENTFUL LIFE

All in all, his was an eventful life,
Humble beginnings, love and strife
In equal measures; a wild, misspent youth,
Drugs, an obscure cult, the search for Truth.
Then Conformity in spades, marriage, two kids
(both cute),a job in the City, a Corporate Suit,
Elevation to the Board, a policy-maker,
A house in the Dordogne, vacations in Jamaica,
Media-attention, a rising star,
A New year;s gong, a mistress in P.R.
Chairman elect following a boardroom coup,
The Charity Commision, inclusion in 'Who's Who';
Divorce (uncontested), mistress becomes wife,
A cardiac condition, the surgeon's knife.
Reflections on Mortality and on Mammon,
Premature retirement, Scottish estate, salmon
Fishing, grouse-shooting, a nouveau Laird,
Forestry, deer-stalking, culling the herd;
Vintage years, myriad memories to evoke,
A mild coronary, then sans warning, a massive stroke.
Family at the bedside, tears, a final embrace,
The monitor straight-lining, of vital signs - no trace.
Funeral, distinguished guests, good food, good wines,
Rememberances shared, eulogies, an obituary
In the Times, the facts in black and white,
The love, the strife, the humble beginnings,
The eventful life.

AUTOBIOGRAPHY OF A HUNTER ELEPHANT
IN A PARALLEL UNIVERSE

That morning
as we trekked
through the bush

my guide
and I were
confronted
by a lone
rogue male.

As soon as
it saw us
we knew
it was going
to charge.

We had
no other choice.

As it came
towards us
I let it
have it
right between
the eyes
with both
barrels

and it
dropped in
its tracks
just a couple
of gunlengths
from where
I was standing.

Approaching it
We discovered
it was still
alive

so my guide
put it out
of its
misery
with a final
single shot
to its
brain.

It was
a fine
specimen
approximately
30 years old
and in its
prime -

a blonde
blue-eyed
human
with all
its own
teeth.

The only
distinguishing
mark a tattoo
on one arm,

a crude
representation
of two
human hearts

symbolically
linked together

and with
the name
'MARY'
scrolled beneath.

Touching.

IN MEMORIAM

for Nimesh Patel

From August until November you hung
In a copse beside the railway line,
Seasoned by the seasons which moved
Around and through you, unseen
By the commuters who passed by
On the hour every hour, en route
To the city you had travelled from so alone.

Then Autumn brought disclosure.
A betrayal of sorts,
Each shed leaf making your discovery
More inevitable, exposing the quiet bower
You had chosen with such care.
Someone walking an unaccustomed path
Finally found you, swaying
Like a Grand Guignol wind-chime
Beneath a sycamore bough.
Found at least what remained
Of you, deciduous You, who shed
Your life with leaf-like ease.

You made the local television News
That day, wedged between
A motorway incident and a report
On corn-circles, filling a four-minute
Slot, the salient facts compressed
To fit into the scheduling.

Does that disappoint you?
Did you expect more, or less?
Possessed by whichever demons
Of Dread that you were,
When the scales finally tipped
And you sought discontinuance

From this world, what did you
Imagine would happen
In the wake of your going?

Perhaps by then you were
Past caring, in free fall, beyond
Any regard for the consequences.
And as you tied the knot
Which held you so safely
Throughout the Summer
And into Autumn, perhaps your
Only thought was for release
From a life which had grown
So intolerable for you.

Downline, those who knew you,
Whose lives were delineated by yours,
Unfold their private maps of grief,
Searching for the co-ordinates
Which might explain the path you took.

Someone should have told you
That nothing stays the same.
Someone should have told you
That humankind is licensed
For pain as much as joy.
Someone should have told you
That the context we call Life
Changes constantly, that the
Permutations are endless,
The possibilities infinite.

The world you knew, dear Nimesh,
Has moved on. Seasons come and go,
Come and go, come and go
Like the trains which still pass daily
By your personal terminus.
Everything has changed
And of course nothing has.
Plus ça change, plus c'est la même chose.

Under the canopy of verdant branches
Which cradled you, Lord Shiva sits
With his necklace of skulls,
Consuming the paradoxes
You tried so hard to understand.
Beneath his divine feet, sycamore roots
Delve deeper into the rich, dark earth,
Searching for stronger anchorage
Against delinquent winds,

Knowing how to hold on
By knowing how to let go.
Knowing how to let go
By knowing how to hold on.

PISCOPHILIA

I know a shoal of
aesthetic piranha
and a trawl
of creative cod,
along with some
spiritual turbot
which have frequent
visions of God.

I correspond weekly
with literate carp
each possessed of
a philosophical bent,
together with
Niechtzean barbel
which live in
the deeps
of the Trent.

I'm acquainted with
a brace of hammerhead
sharks who are decidedly
demi-monde
and a freshwater pike
which acts out fantasies
in a Virtual Reality pond.

I enjoy discourse
with erudite tuna
and composing
belle-canto with pout,
writing haiku
with zen barracuda,
discussing metaphysics
with trout.

All in all
I've a piscatorial
penchant, for fish
of any species
or kind but I'll have
to admit to a definite
preference for those
with an enquiring mind.

APOCALYPSE SOUP
for Bohuslav Barlow

When the Tomorrow which never comes
finally arrives
a 5th generation Apple Mac will develop
an Oedipal Complex
and a Humpback Whale will be elected spokescreature
for the Cetacean Nation at the U.N
Veterans of the Cultural Revolution will perform
in a musical based on the life of Mao
and members of the Royal Family will appear
in an excerpt from 'Private Lives'
at the Royal Command Performance
Traumas will come gift-wrapped
and Infinity will come on Rye
a virus will cause Ultra-Modernist Poets
to shit Neo-Classical Epigrams
and Mystics with Uzis will stalk Fractal Geometrists
and an aubergine purchased at the Paradise Catering Company
in Halifax, West Yorkshire, will, when sliced transversely,
reveal (Peace Be Upon Him) the name of the Prophet.

When the Tomorrow which never comes
finally arrives
a Previously Undefined Psychosis will step out in high heels
and Pope Imelda the First (La Compasionada)
will record a CD of Tibetan Mantras
with digitally-remastered backing tracks by John Lee Hooker
Cooks Tours will offer Virtual Reality Excursions
on the Internet
and Geostationary Satellites will observe and record
demographic trends amongst Primitive Methodists
and the Rapid Eye Movements of Potential Psychopaths
Impotence will be treated by Shamanic Chanting on the NHS
and a virus will calcify human hearts
and the entire text of Das Kapital will be found
in an aubergine bought at a Highgate greengrocer's.

When the Tomorrow which never comes
finally arrives
Margaret Thatcher and Ronald Regan
will be cryogenically revived
and duet together accompanied by the Sons and Daughters
of the Belgrano Victims Tabernacle Choir
Sugar skulls of Pol Pot will be sold through vending outlets
at Ankor Watt, franchised by Khymer Rouge Inc.
and a virus will systematically derange the senses
of Unfrocked Priests
a sheep will be found in Wolf's Clothing
and Innocence will be distilled as a pheromone
the Seven Samurai will clean up the Ginza
and a Pregnant Silence will relate its history
and the entire text of the Bhavagad Gita will be found
in an aubergine purchased in a Bombay store.

When the Tomorrow which never comes
finally arrives
the Information Superhighway will become gridlocked
and the Golden Temple of Amritsar will be wrapped by Christo
MacDonald's will open outlets along the entire length
of the Great Wall of China, items on sale will include
the Big Mao and the Long Munch Burger
thus reducing History to a menu choice
and a geodesic dome will be constructed
over the grassy knoll in Dallas, Texas and paying visitors
will receive commemorative grass clippings
in resin key-chain novelties
in Copenhagen Zoo a human heart
will be transplanted into a baboon called Nancy
and a pop-up edition of the Tibetan Book of the Dead
will be the surpise best-seller at the Frankfurt Book Show
a Koi Carp will be elected to the Japanese Legislature
and Cyberspatial Mortgages will be
offered by Building Societies
and the Declaration of Independence will be found
in an aubergine abandoned in a San Francisco bath-house

When the Tomorrow which never comes
finally arrives
Salman Rushdie, aged 76,will die peacefully in his sleep
surrounded by family, relatives and friends
of his Personal Security Corp.
and using a flame-thrower, a four-year old prodigy
from Kobe, Japan will inscribe haiku by Basho
on slabs of solidified tofu
Jackie Kennedy-Onassis will be beatified by the Vatican
whereupon an order of nuns to be known
as the Little Sisters of the Assassination
will be sanctioned and formed
and a star will appear in the East and Christian leaders will
decide it augers the Second Coming
whereupon three Wise Non-Gender Specific Personages
will fly to Rio de Janiero on unscheduled flights
and lay gifts of Super-conductors, Microchips and DNA
Protein Chains at the feet of a child
born to a transexual cabaret singer,
who conceived after a visitation
by an angel on Copacabana Beach
and an aubergine containing the Complete Works
of the Maquis de Sade will be found
on a park bench in the 13th Androissment, Paris.

When the Tomorrow which never comes
finally arrives
Our Lady of Lourdes will appear twice daily in the Grotto
courtesy of Divine Apparitions Inc.
and Fire-Eating will become an Olympic event
Coca-Cola will sponsor the First Manned Mission to Mars
and a virus will be discovered which engraves pentagrams
on placental walls
the Collective Angst of Industrialized Nations will be caught
masturbating in a dark corner
and Disney will open a theme park in Amazonia
and the entire text of the Torah will be found
in an aubergine purchased in a Brooklyn delicatessen

When the Tomorrow which never comes
finally arrives
a virus which disfigures Public Statuary
will attack the Albert Memorial
and the Old Man of the Internet
will catch a record Cyberfish
and a truffle replicating the exact configuration,
weight and dimensions of Michaelangelo's 'David'
will be found in the Perigord region of France
Spectral Analysis will reveal
that Jackson Pollock painted by numbers
and the Human Genome will finally be mapped
completing the Index of Species
to be published as a paperback by Penguin
The Wimbledon Bicentennial Men's Singles Championship
will be won by a Vertically Challenged Mesomorph
from Puerto Rico
and Cook's Tours will run night-trains to Auschwitz
and the entire text of the Origin of Species
will be discovered in an aubergine left in a Buenos Aires taxi.

When the Tomorrow which never comes
finally arrives
Michelin will publish a Braille map of Route 66
and Damien Hirst will re-create the contents
of Jeffrey Dahmer's freezers at the Tate Gallery
Lovers will throw coins into the waters
Off Chappaquidick Bridge and the Eiffel Tower will
be dismantled and replaced
by a hologram generated from the Jardin de Luxembourg
half-million devotees of the Church of Divine Aerobics
will globally and simultaneously consumate their marriages
and their exertions will be measured on the Richter Scale
and a virus will cause the Spontaneous Amputation
of fingers and toes of Equadorian Virgins
supermarkets will sell Compassion in Aspic
and a bruja in Mexico will make contact with the spirits
of John Lennon and Hogey Carmichael, who will compose
a medley of tunes for the Tijuana Mariachi Co-operative.
and the entire text of the Rosetta Stone will be found

in an aubergine discovered in the Cairo Museum.

When the Tomorrow which never comes
finally arrives
the Final Inundation of Venice will commence
and Holographic Dogs will guide
Visually Disadvantaged Cybernauts
along Virtually Real Streets
a genetically engineered Jabberwock will gyre and gimble
in the wabe, accidentally crushing two onlookers in its abandon
and a convention of Futurists will look back at Everything
and wonder why they hadn't thought of That
a quadriplegic in a Suit of Lights will claim both ears and tail
at the Plaza de Toros, Madrid
and Ziggy Stardust will return with a Zimmer Frame
Dreams will come with a Sell-By Date
and the angelic apparition of William Blake
will cruise Hampstead Heath
and the Aurora Borealis will configure the words
'I CAN'T BREATHE' on behalf of the planet
and an aubergine containing a fully illustrated version
of the Karma Sutra will be found
in the British Museum Reading Room

When the Tomorrow which never comes
finally arrives
Marilyn Monroe will be cloned from a lock of her hair
by a Wisconsin geneticist-fan
and subsequently appear in a remake
of 'Some Like It Hot' co-starring Hugh Grant and Johnny Depp
and Primate Development Inc. will offer genetically
enhanced chimpanzees for domestic service
Psycho-Kinetic Toys will be sold at Hamleys
and a virus which induces narcpoleptic states will be developed
and used to facilitate better inmate control
in Penal Institutions
Guilt will come vacuum-packed
and the I-Ching will be available on CD Rom
and the entire text of The Interpretation of Dreams
will be found in an aubergine in a Viennese restaurant

When the Tomorrow which never comes
finally arrives
the Meek shall inherit the Earth and form a company
registered at Lloyd's as Humility Inc.
and a virus which skips a generation will do just that
Rupert Murdoch will look Death in the face
and make Him/Her an offer for Terrestrial Rights
and the Hammer of Africa will beat
upon the Anvil of Europe
Cyberpriests will celebrate marriages on the Internet
and suicide notes will be left on e-mail
a minotaur will run amok in a shopping mall
and Mr Average will return to his suburban home and discover
a satyr copulating with his wife
the Final Days of the Defence of Saigon will be re-staged
by veterans of the campaign travelling in Huey helicopters
courtesy of Cook's Historical Tours
and transgeneticists will create a potato which will taste
like Beef Bourguignon and aubergines
which taste like aubergines.

When the Tomorrow which never comes
finally arrives
the New Luddites, an extremist
anti-technology group will disrupt
the Internet with a virus which causes dyslexia amongst users
and Cyberwhales will feed on the Krill of Human Dreams
I.D. cards will be replaced by sub-dermal bar-code
Karma Gamblers will use Loaded Dice
and the New Society For Cutting Up Men
will apply to the Vatican
for the beatification of Valerie Solanis
Elvis Presley will be found alive and well and living
in a Retirement Home in Boise, Idaho
and an Abyss of Biblical Proportions
will open up in Central Park, N.Y.
the Colonic Irrigation of Large Mammals
will become a spectator sport
and the American Dream will only be screened
in Black and White

36

Damien Hirst will exhibit the post-mortem remains
Of motorway crash-victims at his first Retrospective
and Chanel will sell a range of silk purses made from sow's ears
and a Great White Shark caught off the Great Barrier Reef
will be found to contain the remains of
Lord Lucan, Captain Oates, Josef Mengele,
Jimmy Hoffa and Shergar
and an aubergine which contains the complete text
of the Rights of Man

and a Bird in the Hand will become worth ten in a bush
and Here and There will become There and Then
and there will be Immaculate Conceptions
and Immaculate Misconceptions
and wolves will scavenge along the Champs d'Elysees
and the Valkyries will ride through the Brandenburg Gate
and there will be bread queues outside Harrods
and a questionnaire will arrive
from the Apocalypse Provision Company
and Benedictine monks will burn in city squares
and snowflakes will fall in triple configurations
auguring the arrival of the Great Beast
and a virus will infect politicians with the Truth
and the Inevitable will happen Again and Again
and Worms everywhere Will Turn
and the consumption of the Whole Enchilada will commence
and the Fat Lady will start to sing
and Enough Will Be Just That

and just before the Balance is finally
and irrevocably tipped
Text Empathic Vegetables of Indeterminable Classification,
but. somewhat resembling aubergines
and containing the entire text of this poem
will be found in libraries throughout the world

when the Tomorrow
which never comes
finally arrives.

HOW TO CATCH AN ANGEL
for Mercedes

First,

find a quiet corner
of Infinity.

Somewhere off
the beaten track,

away from
the Trade Routes

of those
who deal
in souls.

For bait
use the Possibility
of Redemption.

Then wait.

An aeon
or two
is not unusual.

If by then
you have not
heard the sound
of approaching
wings,

other lures
should be
employed.
Pheromones

of Supressed
Guilt,

of Contrition,
of Desire
for Salvation,

should draw
one from
its Celestial
Perch.

When one
finally appears

you must
act swiftly

Move forward
quietly whilst intoning
a prayer.

Something
of Undeniable Piety

always does
the trick.

And while
it stands,
listening,

mesmerised
by the Utter
Sanctity
of the moment,

reach out
and from
its enfolded
wings,
gently pluck
a feather.

One will
be enough -

for thus
no longer
Immaculate

it will have
to stay
with you

forever.

BOUNCERS

They stand guard
in the doorways
of the laser-lit
tabernacles
of delight,

deciding nightly
who amongst
the Spandex multitudes
will be denied entry
or who will pass,

dark archangels
in slick tuxedoes,
beneath which
beat hearts

of pure brass.

LAKE

Because there is no wind today
You lie, serene as an old dog,
Beneath a neutral sky.
Caught now in earth's natural
Pose, our mutual silences
Acknowledge your perfection.

With you there is no mask.
You are simply what you are,
Water which sat down and stayed
To delight occasional vagrant eyes.

In you, elemental milk, the world
Distils it's favorite images.
Effortlessly you twin the sun
And mark it's ancient strut,
Stars flare, clouds soar and pass.
Softly you parody the changing moon
Whilst at your edge the seasons
Rework their schemes.

Small stones are enough
To shatter your calm, but today
There are no stones - today
It is the noon traffic
Of three ducks and a solitary
Boatman, his oars creasing
Your face with surreal intent.

NINETEEN SIXTY THREE

Returning home
unexpectedly from
a promotional tour
of the Midlands

he surprised his wife
in their bed
with her lover.

Walked straight in
on them, entering
their dark bower
just as she came

and just as the news
was breaking
on the portable
in the corner
of the room,

which presumably
they had been watching
before turning to play
the two-backed beast.

Even now,
more than three
decades later

he often reflects
on the colossal
coincidentally
of the moment

and still recalls
her piglet squeals
counterpointing

the elegiac tones
of the newscaster
who was announcing
to the world

that the golden-haired,
philosopher-prince
of the West,

the President,
was dead.

STORM DAMAGE

Last night the world was awash
With wind and rain and while
My significant others slept,
Wrapped in their innocences
And dreams, I lay awake until
The storm blew itself out and
Listened to the old house complain.

Now in morninglight we can see
What damage has been done.
Less actually than expected.
The only testament
To the frenzy heard the night
Before are the remains
Of slates lifted from the roof
And flung down, shattered,
Token damage, nothing more.

Darling, so much depends upon
The weather. The expedition to
The Matto Grosso and the fate
Of the Vicarage fête are equally
Dependent upon its vagaries.

So we watch clouds, indict sunrises
And sunsets, measure rainfall,
Record wind-speeds, temperatures,
Humidities, observe the behaviour
Of animals and listen
With congregational reverence
To daily forecasts.

The need to know what blows
Our way, is understandable.
Forewarned is foreamed.
But our only certainty
Is Uncertainty itself.

Just when we think we have
Everything under control
Reality enters from the wings
Carrying a bouquet of delusions.

If a metaphor were needed
To describe our lives,
The most apt would describe
Us in terms of weather;
Deluge, torrent, blast, squall,
Turbulence, occlusion, trough,
Depression, highs and lows.

The remains of last night's
Stürm-fest are cleared away;
Gathered, swept-up, disposed of.

A patch of blue eases through
The dark cloud-shrouded sky.

On the gable end, dog roses
Twitch like exposed nerves
In the softening breeze.

The roof will be repaired.

AVATAR'S REPORT

The timing was all wrong.
Arriving when I did
It was little wonder
My manifestation went un-noticed.

An incandescent descent
In a chariot of burnished gold,
Pulled by a brace of chimera,
Would have, under normal circumstances
Generated the desired level of awe
And fearful reverence to be expected
From beings of their intelligence.

But with the level of planetary activity
And spectacle encountered,
My appearance to say the least
Seemed *passé.*

It should be noted that future
Interventions should first be preceded
By in-depth socio-cultural
And religious screening to ensure

That any incarnation does not
Occur synchronously with events
Such as bi-millennial celebrations

In remembrance of the birth
Of a minor Messianic figure.

TWENTY-FIVE REASONS WHY
ALBERT RIO VASQUEZ JNR. DIED

Because someone had to draw a line somewhere
Because LeRoy went
Because you could get your kicks on Route 66,
but who knew what kicks
you could get on the Road to Hanoi
Because Rooster Cockburn said 'Go for your guns,you
sons of a bitch!'
Because the Geopolitical Stability of the World was at risk
Because it might be, it might just be the Wildest Trip ever
Because Charlie was rubbing our faces in it, but good
Because she said guys in uniform made her feel really horny
Because Jagger couldn't get no Satisfaction
Because Billy Lee called me a wuss
Because no one, but no one tells Uncle Sam what to do
Because the surf was up Dude and some waves you just
gotta ride
Because of the joint we shared that night in Johannson's barn
Because the buck caught in the cross-hairs of a telescopic sight
was no longer enough
Because Poppa Had A Brand New Bag
Because Uncle Linus said Korea had been a real gas
Because 'What's a brother to do - Whitey's Out there havin'
all the fun'
Because Proof Needed To Be Given Through The Night
Because the whores in Saigon are just the Best ever and
they'll go down on you for the price of a beer
Because 'there ain't no right and there ain't no wrong -
there's just things we do'
Because of the Daughters of the American Revolution
Because those goddam Gooks hadda be stopped, just hadda
Because violence is the last resort of an exhausted mind
Because Good Ol' Boys Were Drinkin' Whiskey an' Rye
Because God was on our side

LAZARUS TALKING

In the harbour a freighter waits for the tide,
Lights in constellation against the skyline.
I do not sleep well.
Rats scutter on the wharf below
And the lap of water is ceaseless.
Tomorrow perhaps I shall leave.
Move South for the winter
With the birds and the migrant rich.

Nothing holds me here.
Time neuters all emotions.
My latest toy sirs beside me in bed.
She turns as a child turns in sleep
With their cargo of innocence.
Her breasts have brought me no comfort.
I straddled her indifferently,
Matching her counterfeit ecstasy with mine.
Daybreak will see her gone,
Bright as a macaw
To her street-corner perch.

At times like these Martha,
I often think of you
And of our childhood in the olive-groves.
And thinking of you long to ask
Why did you ask the Nazarene to breathe
Life into me again?
Was it grief or sheer perversity of love
Which made you act?
One lifetime is enough for anyone

Now, his mule of History,
His walking-talking miracle,
I wonder, am I vital to a plan
Or a forgotten relic in his side-show?
I would prosper in a carnival.
The unbelievable is always rare.

With my Byzantine eyes and nuclear smile,
His freak, I'd knock 'em dead.

Sleep well dear shade,
Dear sister, sleep well.
Across the straits the wind rides in
With alien scents to excite unseasoned hearts.
In the deeps between
Dolphins course beneath the rising sea.
Onward, forever moving forward.
Who is their Messiah?

Incline your ear sweet Jesus,
Your monster speaks.
Is it too much to ask?
Throw the switch
And let my antique heart wind down.

My papers are all in order.

SALMON FARM

All they will
ever know
is this Belsen
of nets

which contains
them

and the sun's
passage

across
a variable
quadrant of sky

and vagrant
clouds

and the moon
in all its phases

and a flux
of stars
welding
a fragment

of the Universe
above them

and prodigal
hands scattering manna

onto dark,
benevolent waters.

FOUNTAINS ABBEY

Piety honed the blades
which cut and shaped these stones.
Raised in God's name
eight centuries ago, they stand
less substantial now than once
they were,but still sublime –
each one consecrated
by the sun which shines
on them today

and on the visiting throngs
who Kodak their moments
as they pass and speak

in tongues.

IDENTITY PARADE

Sheer chance brought me here.
When They stopped me in the street
And asked me to take part in the proceedings,
I naturally complied. Like any good citizen
I recognize my civic duty when it comes along.
Besides They were Civility itself
And as my dear old Mum used to say,
There's no substitute for good manners.

So here I am, shoulder to shoulder
With a motley crew all similar in build
And complexion to yours truly.
Most of them, are like myself participating
By request, but there are those
Who are obviously making an appearance,
Less than willingly.
They stand, tense with practised insouciance,
Their expressions clichés of innocence,
Past masters of the blank stare, exuding
Duplicity from every socially deprived pore.

We wait beneath a probe of lights, facing
The smoked-glass screen behind which
The victim will be standing with the investigating officers.
At least one of them will be female;
Softly- spoken, reassuring, empathic;
There to support the victim
Through the ordeal of attempting to identify
The animal who raped her earlier today.

She will not succeed. How can she
When she did not see Him?
What can she tell?
Only the details she will hate to re-live.

If only now she could walk along
The line as victims once did

She might recognize
The aftershave her attacker wore.

It is very distinctive.
I go to great lengths to obtain it.
I buy it in memory of my Mum,
Who brought me my first bottle
Back from Italy after a coach-tour
To Lake Como.

I'm wearing it now.
She cannot smell it, but I smell her.
Her scents linger on my clothes, her sweat,
Her fear, the pheromones of Terror
She released whilst I occupied her territory.
I hear her too, despite her sound-proof sanctuary.
I have her every cry, her every whimper,
The soundtrack of our little téte a téte
Inside my head

Presumably, we shall be able to leave shortly.
I do believe there's a fee for the assitance
rendered and the inconvenience suffered.
I shall donate it to the Little Sisters of Mercy.
They were so kind to you Mum, during
Your final travail. Sleep tight Darling.
One day we shall be together once more.
I shall join you on the distant shore
I imagine you waiting on.
Good-night. God bless

I have kept the promise I made you.
No woman holds dominion over me,
But every man has his needs.

I know you understand.

TOTEM

A caul of shadows.

Stones from Auschwitz
illuminated under neon.

Ploughshares turning
furrows of blood.

Desires weeping
in an abyss.

Chinook nosing upstream
through melt-water surges.

Orchids flowering
between neural synapses.

A conclave of satyrs
drinking from
placental crucibles.

Copulating moths trapped
in fragments of amber.

Nautilus shells
superimposed over
pubescent breasts.

A full moon caught
In the sycamore's
dark net.

CHAOS THEORY

for the Lopez Woman

Querida, if ever Fate should decide
To take you somehow from my side

My howl of loss would reverberate
Around the world and devastate

All that stood within its path
With a hurricane's power and wrath

Laying waste vast tracts of land
Reducing verdance to desert sand

Simultaneously setting into motion
Tectonic plates beneath an ocean

Whose stirrings would then create
Tidal waves which would inundate

Towns and cities on a global scale
Where epidemics would soon prevail

From which a virulent plague would spread
Traversing continents and leaving dead

Pyred high in each and every nation
A truly apocalyptic decimation

From which Anarchy would rampage
Plunging the world into a New Dark Age

At the epicentre of which would be
The hollow shell which once was me

Querida, should ever Fate decide
To take you somehow from my side.

CRASH

For those with a taste
for statistics, the impact speed
was estimated at 60mph
and blood-alcohol levels
exceeded 250 units per milligramme.

For those with a taste
for the sensational, the driver was
found with his trousers
around his ankles, whilst
his passenger was found kneeling
next to him, naked to her waist.

For those with a taste
for the understatement
a police spokesperson commented
"the victims were apparently indulging
in practices not commensurate
with safe driving........"

For those with a taste
for the poetic, the drystone wall
they smashed into
remains unrepaired

the gap created,
a kind of memorial
between which moor grasses
and clouds

inscribe
transient epitaphs.

PERFECT DAY

What has happened
To the wind?

Have the trees
Petrified overnight?

Have the birds
Taken a vow
Of silence?

Across the valley
Not one cloud,

Not one whisp
Of white

Mars the sky's
Absolute blue
Template.

Nothing moves.
Nothing sounds.
It's ominous.

Why is the earth
Holding its breath?

I need something
To disturb
This perfect
October morning.

Something.
Anything.
Some small turmoil

In order
To maintain

My equilibrium.

Check me out on the Net. I'm there
In all my glory. Though some people might
Find it all a little too gory,
I survive there - sliced transversely
From head to foot.

It's a kind of immortality.
My usual visitors are academics,
Medical students pathologists
And the morbidly curious.
But there are others.
An old lady in Albequerque visits me
Every day. She likes to leaf through
The sections of my heart.
Why she does it is impossible to say.
I sense grief. It's touching in its way.

Likewise, the kid from Yonkers
Who hits the site on a daily basis too.
Even though he appears to have a fixation
About my urino-genital system, I look
Forward to his visits along with those
Of the Neo-Abstract Expressionist in Dresden
Who bases all his work on the disposition
Of my viscera and the girl in Kyoto
Who composes Karmic haiku
Whilst she scrolls through me.
With others they form an extended family,
Posthumous of course.

Looking at the situation analytically
You might say my execution
Has been extremely productive.
Justice has been served and in death
I serve a purpose.
There's a balance in that I find pleasing.

Once I was a loser, but now
I'm a model citizen,

Cyberspatially speaking.

SMALL MILLENNIUM SONG

Everybody's talking Apocalypse,
Armageddon's on everybody's lips.
It's a sign of the times
In this Time of Signs.

Somebody's thrown a malevolent rune,
Media prophets are predicting doom.
It's a sign of the time
In this Time of Signs

Rationality's been blown to bits,
Everybody's got the Millennium shits.
It's a sign of the times
In this Time of Signs.

Wholesale angst is what's downloading,
Mystics are seismic with foreboding.
It's a sign of the times
In this Time of Signs.

Something out there's out to harm us,
Everybody's reading Nostrodamus.
It's a sign of the times
In this Time of Signs.

Genocides, plagues ,cataclysms,
Despair, doubts, religious schisms.
It's a sign of the times
In this Time of Signs.

But it's not over by a long chalk yet,
I'm sending out a message on the Internet.
Getting on-line
In this Time of Signs.

Message reads: Don't give up the ghost.
Celebrate Life with those you love most.
Take it down the line
In this Time of Signs.

Because Love survives, come what may.
So give it what you've got till Judgement Day:
And let its fierce light shine
In this Time of Signs.

IN SPATE

After a night of rain
The river is in spate.
Wild water, dark with loam
Shorn from the moors;
An arterial gush from the groin
Of the peat-god who resides
On the bleak heights
Above the town

On streets as slick as vinyl,
Hunched figures lean into obligue drizzle
Or hurry by under umbrellas opened
Against graphite-coloured clouds,
Oblivious to the congregation of ducks
Which have sought refuge beneath
A hump-backed bridge
And stand contemplating the torrent
With the tranquility
Of Zen masters.

A childhood ago, on rafts
Of dreams I sailed endless rivers
Endlessly. Huck Finned imagined
Mississippis, relentlessly setting course
For the adventures
Which always lay downstream

And summered on riverbanks
With my brother, camping overnight
To rise at dawn and fish first light,
Waiting for the bite which would
Bring the ultimate specimen
To the readied net.

Dear days held deep in memory.
Time Past when the world was rich
With possibilities and certainties

Danced as brightly as mayflies.

But between then and now, oceans
Of water have flowed beneath bridges.
And as I watch this day's surge
Scourge buttressed stone, I know
Only this, my dark dove.

Our lives are like rivers
And we go wherever our vagrant souls
Take us, never knowing
What lies around the next bend,
Borne away by currents
We can never comprehend.

HUMPHREY BOGART

'Reports of my death are greatly exaggerated...'

It seemed natural for you
To go the way you did,
Laconic to the end, spitting
An epitaph through tight lips,
Smoke wreathing your
Houndog face.

Between celluloid postures,
Entirely human, you found
Life sufficient filled by friends,
Chess, booze and a woman
Who could whistle
When she needed you

Content finally to let
The latest chronic hero
Saunter across the screen
Into the improbable situation,

When it came
Death was nothing new,
You'd died a hundred
Times before.

What I want to know is
What gods do you hustle now?
And to what black angel
Do you growl 'Play it again, Sam'

Or words to that effect.

AUGUST

We open
the door
to a votive
offering,

a small, sleek,
perfectly dead,
unblemished
shrew

which a
neighbourhood cat,

obviously wishing
to placate
some feline
deity,

has left
on the smooth
stone

altar

of our
doorstep

STARRY NIGHT AT CASA HERNANDEZ
for Alma and Silvia, Washington DC 1999

Midnight early August
And in the Hockney blue water
Of an illuminated rooftop pool
The children sport like dolphins,
While the two of you sit, talking,
Making up for fifteen years
Of separation, resurrecting
Memories wholesale;
Births, deaths, marriages,
Adulteries, divorces -
Bartering them like traders
At the end of a long voyage.

All around us the lights
Of Washington burn
Like supplicant's candles
Left at a colossal shrine
And above us the stars
Have aligned themselves
Into familiar configurations.

O noche luminoso!
Night of bright water,
Of bright city streets,
Of blazing constellations!

Compared with stellar existences
Our lives are as brief
As summer butterflies.

But Love abides.
Love endures.

Endures longer than
The shooting star
seeking earthfall
As you talk,

An orphan fragment
Blazing briefly, curving
Downward over Capitol Hill
In celebration
Of your reunion.

PTA DANCE / RECHERCHE DU TEMPS PERDUE

It's sad watching the Children
Of the Revolution, dance.
So sad, watching Fortysomethings
In kaftans and crushed velvet loons,
Swaying on stack-heels
To the sounds of a retro-DJ.

I should not have come.
Nostalgia is dangerous
In small doses.
Is as potent as hashish.

Now I shall not sleep tonight
But ride again with her sleeping head
On my shoulder, while the moon
Rises over the mountain
Like a communion host
On the rim of a chalice
And the scent of bougainvillea
Pervades the air
On the midnight 'bus

From Tangier
To Marrakesh.

CYNIC'S SONNET

Do not put your trust in Love.
Do not. Put your trust in Love
And it will break your heart
As surely as night follows day
Love will break your heart someway.

Do not put your trust in Love.
Do not. Put your trust in love
And as surely as day follows night
Love will lift you up, then let you
Fall from its blind height.

Someday, someway Love will find
A way to break your heart in two,
The way that Love is bound to do,
If you put your trust in Love.

STIGMATA

It was Monday
and she was taking advantage

of the special
discounts on offer
for one week only
at the Hypermarket.

Her palms
began bleeding
as she examined
the early broccoli

and the wound in her side
opened up
in the dairy
produce section

contaminating
a selection
of cheeses
as she chose
some brié.

The manager
was summoned
by concerned
members of staff

and he informed her
that in view of the fact
that the store

was not licensed
for the retail
of blood products

and that quasi-
religious, in-store
manifestations
were strictly against
company policy

she would
have to vacate
the premises.

STORMWATCHING AT MAHI MAH'S

Beneath agitated ceiling fans
We watch thunderheads build up
Out over the Atlantic,
Growing darker as they approach,
Swelling like time-lapse tumours.

A sudden gust shakes
The blue canopy above our heads
And the sky turns slate-grey.

Unable to resist the earth's lure
Clouds discharge their caches
Of electricity, vivid slashes of light
Followed by thunder

Which sounds just as the waiter
Brings Mexican beer and oysters
And a lone pelican dives one last time
Before taking off on a lazy search
For some sanctuary inland.

Everyone and everything needs
A place to run to, my love,
A place of shelter.
How many times have I come to you
When Life has worn me down?
How many times have I sailed to safety
Into the tender harbour of your arms?

While I breathe, never leave me.
Without you I could not weather
The storms which blow me
Every which way.

Now the rain comes.
Off-shore dark fins rise,
Slicing through turbulent waters,

A pod of dolphins
Running parallel to the police car
Which cruises like a shark
Along the boardwalk,
Its red light turning, turning,
Informing us that the storm
Has finally arrived.

NOCTURNE

Summoned by a hunter's moon
An owl, on hypersilent wings
Drifts over meadows beyond the house,
Husking shadows as its brings
Armageddon to the mouse.

FILM NOIR

She was trouble from the start
I knew the moment we met;
Trouble with a capital 'T'.
It was the way she lit her cigarette
And the way she looked at me.

She was trouble from the start
I knew the moment we met;
Trouble in spades, y'know the kind.
Come-on eyes, stacked up top,
One look and she blew my mind.

She was trouble from the start
I knew the moment we met;
Said she'd just blown in from Chi,
That some gunzel was on her tail.
Should've known it was a lie.

She was trouble from the start,
I knew the moment we met;
Things were just too sweet.
Forgot to check her out -
Should've known she was packing heat.

She was trouble from the start,
I knew from the moment we met;
I knew it'd end like this,
The expected betrayal amongst shadows,
The bullet, the final kiss.

HARLEM GLOBETROTTERS

Gazelles and clowns in coordination
They pass effortlessly, one, beyond
The lucrative hand, gravity conceding
To their art, the sway, the swerve,
The ball lobbed high and accurate:
Geometry of muscle and eye moving
For the joy of it, miming as they go
The heart's punchline in glad pattern,
Intricate, bloodful black ballet

DANCE CLASS

Un-sylphlike in regimented pink
My daughter tutus her way
Across the dance-school floor.

Gathered with her class-mates
She watches, trying to memorize
A demonstrated sequence
As the pianist in a corner
Tampers with a Chopin etude.

Assembled, readied, they start to dance;
Gracefully awkward, awkwardly graceful.
A tulled platoon on manoeuvres,
A gaggle of apprentice flamingoes,
Almost moving in unison.

Poised, they stare straight ahead,
Mesmerized by their doppelgangers
Reflected in the unforgiving mirrors
Which line the studio walls.

Seven dancers doubled
Choreographing their dreams,
As they move together -
A collective heartbeat
Away from absolute perfection.

POMEGRANATES

Squat and unyeilding, they
Resemble crude grenades, are
Hard to the touch, waxen-skinned
With no promise of succulence.
Only when a knife is taken
To them do they surrender
Their riches, their rosy plenitude.

As children we ate them
Using pins to spear each individual
Delicate, soft, pink seed-pearl,
Making one fruit last,
A whole day or more.

Now one, an impulse purchase
Resides in my kitchen, reposing in
A basketful of conspiritorial apples,
A small bomb of Remembrance,
Daring me to eat it

But I have learned to wait,
For the right moment,
Always bearing in mind
That detonating memories
Can be expensive

And that casualties
Are not always avoidable.

MEDITATION

Late Autumn night.
I had gone outside to close
The yard-gate left agape
by a departed friend.
And not watching
Where I put my feet
I stepped upon the snail
Which just at that
Precise moment
Was slowly traversing
My dark path.

The shell disintegrated
Beneath my tread.
Its divine architecture
Crushed beyond all repair,
Its fragile remains littering
The viscous sliver which had
Been its recent occupant.

What will happen now?

If a tree falling in a rainforest
Might cause a tidal wave
To break upon shores
A continent away,
What disaster might I
Have loosed upon the world?

What might this
Casual holocaust breed?
What might arise now
From the gothic equations
Of Chaos?

What pain ensue?
What blood?

All because I did not
Take care where
I stood?

RELIC

One by one, the supplicants
Approach the altar-rail
In order to kiss
The domed-glass cover
Of the container beneath
Which the severed hand
Of a minor English
Martyr resides.

Each kiss is an act
Of Faith, an act of Hope
That a cure might
Be affected.

Kiss-for a heart condition.
Kiss-for a tumour.
Kiss-for a seizure.

And after each kiss
The glass is wiped clean.
Kiss-wipe. Kiss-wipe.
Kiss-wipe. Kiss-wipe.

Even in the pursuit
Of miracles, standards
Of hygiene

Have to be maintained.

FASHION VICTIM'S PRAYER

Our *Prada*, who art in fashion
Hallowed be thy Style.
Thy *Calvin Klein* come,
Thy will be done,
In *Umbro*,
Addidas in heaven.
Give us this day
Our daily *Benetton*
And forgive us our *Reeboks*,
As we forgive those
Who *Reebok* against us,
For *Nike* is the Kingdom,
The *Puma* and the *Gucci*,
Forever and ever,

Armani.

LINES ON NON-ALCOHOLIC WINES AT SAINSBURY'S

Between the Liebfraumilch
and the Chilean Pinot Noir
they extend their
pale green necks,

bottles of moral rectitude,
the vintner's equivalent
of non-penetrative sex.

FLOWERING CHERRY

Effortlessly in the volatile season
You appear, soft pink detonation.
Not for you the rose's anger
Or the trepidation of the lily.

Elusive you promise nothing
Except perhaps some peace
For the paupered lens
And for the soul, soft fingering
Over old scars.

GENESIS : UNAUTHORISED VERSION

From the beginning
it is essential
to get things
absolutely right.
Nothing less
will do.

Being meticulous
He commences
with the Darkness,

illuminating it
with a galaxy here
a nebula there,
scattering stars,
planets, moons
asteroids, comets, meteors...

a Void seeded,
a Cosmos
set into motion

impressive
prestidigitation,
even for a Deity.

Phase Two requires
more attention to detail
requires a miniaturist's art,
a midwife's touch.

He etches continents
on terrestrial masses,
pleats mountain ranges,
scours plains, furrows
valleys, gouges out
river-beds in readiness

for the Deluge
He causes to fall,
forming in the process
the oceans and the seas.

Whereupon
He sets upon the earth,
and in the waters
and in the skies

creatures great
and small
to populate
the vastness,

after which
in order
to complete
His *magnum opus*,
He takes
a handful of clay
and breathes
into it

kindling
Humanity
and shaping it
in His image.

Then reaching out
(without moving
of course,

omnipresence
being yet another
talent in his extensive
repertoire)

He removes a rib
from the Man
and fashions from it,
Woman.

Perfection!
Absolute Perfection.

But as He is
about to take
a well-earned rest
something
in the Universe,
His Universe

stirs restlessly,
shifts uneasily,

and this *something*
informs Him
that Humankind
Just won't be able
to handle
absolute perfection.

So without
further ado
He transports
them both
to a wondrous
Garden of Delights

(which He had
prepared earlier)

and before leaving
Them To work things out

He creates
in the Wornan

an insatiable desire

for
Forbidden Fruit.

And having done
That, finally
leaves them
alone

and goes off
to await
developments.

WIRED

There's something wrong
with my heart.

Every now and then
it decides to beat
less regularly
than it should.

Every now and then
it beats out a mambo
instead of a waltz.

Every now and then
it feels as if
there's a small bird
trapped in my chest,
seeking release.

So I lay back,
compliant as a lab rat
while they wired me up,

attached electrodes to me
in order to record
my heart's machinations,

in order that those
who can read
electronic runes
and decipher
the hieroglyphics
of cardio-vascular
activities

would be in possession
of all the facts,
so that no clinical stone
would be left unturned.

But as they wired me up,
I couldn't hellp thinking
over and over
and over again...

Where are the machines
which can chronicle
the Secret Lives
of our hearts?

Where are the machines
which can read
the heart's memories?

Where are the machines
which can register
those moments
that make all
the difference?

Like the seismic morning
you walked into Judy's
where I was reading
the paper by the window

and our life
together
began.

HISTORY

While her husband and children
gather around the hospital bed.
waiting for the inevitable,
she lies naked in a cornfield
with a farmboy from the mid-West,
her GI lover who is only 48 hours
from death on a Normandy beach.

And as she lies there, feeling joyously
brazen and abandoned, absolutely certain
that they will live happily ever after,
the faultless blue sky they lie beneath
tips sideways and she slips painlessly
into the brightness beyond, leaving
her husband and children wondering
what she could possibly have meant
when she whispered

"Idaho..."

OLD MEN PLAYING TENNIS

Between them they've clocked up
A century and a half
And are a living, breathing
Testament to the triumph
Of socialised medicine.

Diabetes, a replaced hip,
A colostomy and shared hypertension
Have not diluted their enthusiasm
For the game they play now
In the late Spring sunlight.

And although overhead smashes
Are no longer part
Of their stroke repertoire
And their long game
Has long since suffered abbreviation,
Every ball is still competed for.
Every ball, even though
They've ceased to keep score.

Winning is no longer their motivation.
Their only imperitive is to compete
And to play on regardless of the fact
That Death is calling all the shots
And making all the calls.

Every serve made is an affirmation.
Every return, a triumph.
In off-white whites
They ghost around the court,
Their shadows dancing on the red shale,
And in that choreography
Something indominatable,
Can be glimpsed, some *something*
Which eludes exact definition.

WITHOUT MAPS

We come
into this world
without a map.

We leave
this world
without a map.

And between
our Entrance
and our Exit

we make
countless journeys
without maps.

Journeys
for which
no cartographer
has ever drawn
a map.

Not Michelin.
Not Ordinance Survey.
Not Amerigo Vespucci.
Not even Mercator
with his wonderful
projection.

Forget all of them.

Mere calculators
of distances.

Mere cataloguers
of destinations,

describers
of oceans
and seas,

of deserts
and rainforests

of mountain ranges
and rivers

of countries
and continents

useful only
when we need
to travel
from A to B.

Some journeys
have no
co-ordinates.

Some journeys
are beyond
reference

to latitude
and longitude.

Those journeys
which can
only be made

by the heart's
dead reckoning.

Navigations
only possible
using

the dark compass
of the soul.